33 WAYS TO RAISE YOUR CREDIT SCORE

33 WAYS

TO RAISE YOUR

CREDIT SCORE

PROVEN STRATEGIES
TO IMPROVE YOUR CREDIT
AND GET OUT OF DEBT

TOM CORSON-KNOWLES

Get the free newsletter for more financial freedom tips at:

www.blogbusinessschool.com

Published by TCK Publishing:

www.tckpublishing.com

Earnings Disclaimer

When addressing financial matters in any of our books, sites, videos, newsletters or other content, we've taken every effort to ensure we accurately represent our products and services and their ability to improve your life or grow your business. However, there is no guarantee that you will get any results or earn any money using any of our ideas, tools, strategies or recommendations, and we do not purport any "get rich schemes" in any of our content. Nothing in this book is a promise or guarantee of earnings. Your level of success in attaining similar results is dependent upon a number of factors including your skill, knowledge, ability, dedication, business savvy, network, and financial situation, to name a few. Because these factors differ according to individuals, we cannot and do not guarantee your success, income level, or ability to earn revenue. You alone are responsible for your actions and results in life and business. Any forward-looking statements outlined in this book or on our Sites are simply our opinion and thus are not guarantees or promises for actual performance. It should be clear to you that by law we make no guarantees that you will achieve any results from our ideas or models presented in this book or on our Sites, and we offer no professional legal, medical, psychological or financial advice.

CONTENTS

WHY YOU SHOULD READ THIS BOOK

The truth is, there's a lot of bogus information out there about credit scores. I had challenges with credit card debt and a low credit score early in life and I don't want anyone else to have to struggle like I did.

I've spent years researching credit scores and have several years of experience in the debt collection and credit card industry. In this book, you will find only accurate, clear and helpful information to help you improve your credit score and get out of debt.

Not only will you learn about how the FICO credit score formula works, but you'll learn 33 quick and simple ways you can immediately improve your credit score.

Some of these strategies are so simple that you could improve your credit score by 20-30 points with just one of these strategies in just a single day. Other strategies may take time to pay off, but can be very rewarding.

Whether you're trying to get out of debt, qualify for a better rate on your mortgage or auto loan, or just want to take better care of your finances, this book will help.

You won't find any fluff, jargon or confusing language in here. Just real, helpful down-to-earth facts about how to improve your credit score and take back control of your financial life.

Here's to your success!

Tom Corson-Knowles

THE BENEFITS OF A GOOD CREDIT SCORE

M ost people think a credit score is just a nice thing to have, but good credit can do a lot more than you might think.

A good credit score is an asset you can use in many ways to save you a lot of money, time, energy and effort.

The average American could save thousands of dollars a year simply by improving their credit score. Here's how...

LOWER INTEREST RATES ON CREDIT CARDS AND LOANS

Interest rates are determined in large measure by your credit score. Having a higher credit score can dramatically lower your interest rates on credit cards and loans, meaning potentially thousands of dollars in savings. You can use all that saved money from lower interest to pay down debt, save for your child's education and for retirement. Now that's smart financial management!

Simply by managing your credit score better, you can reduce your interest rates, save thousands of dollars, use those extra savings to pay down debt, and get ahead financially. Over a 10, 20, 30 or 40 year timeline, those savings on interest alone could be the difference between you owning your home free and clear and going through foreclosure.

EASIER LOAN AND CREDIT CARD APPROVAL

If you have a low credit score, it can be difficult to get accepted for a loan, mortgage or credit card. Having an excellent credit score doesn't guarantee approval, but it greatly increases your chances. If you're looking to buy a new home or car anytime in the next few years, it's important to start improving your credit score starting right now.

GET APPROVED FOR HIGHER LIMITS

Your borrowing capacity is based on your income and your credit score. With a good credit score, banks are willing to let you borrow more money because you've demonstrated that you pay back what you borrow on time. If you do get approved with a bad credit score, you'll probably only be approved for a small amount, which may not be enough to accomplish your goals.

BETTER NEGOTIATING POWER

With a good credit score, you can often negotiate a lower interest rate on your credit card or a new loan. When you have great credit, most companies will work with you to offer better terms, knowing that you will be a good customer who pays their bills on time.

Don't be afraid to negotiate hard with good credit! Just as much as you need a loan, banks and credit card companies need new customers. Feel free to play one bank or offer against another to get the best deal possible for you. But you can't do that as effectively without a strong credit score for bargaining power.

EASIER TO RENT

Most landlords check your credit history as part of the standard rental application screening process. Many landlords will gladly accept an applicant with good credit and will do whatever they can to avoid applicants with bad credit. If you're looking for a good place to rent, you better make sure you have good credit.

LOWER CAR INSURANCE RATES

Car insurance companies will give huge discounts to customers with good credit. Having bad credit can increase your insurance rates by as much as $100 or more. Insurance companies say that people with bad credit tend to file more claims are therefore penalized with a higher insurance premium. What would you do with a few hundred dollars?

CELL PHONE BENEFITS

If you have poor credit, many cell phone service providers will not give you a contract. You might have to choose a pay-as-you-go plan and pay much more for your cell phone. On the other hand, customers with good credit have no problem getting a cell phone service contract and tend to get great discounts on phones as well, which could mean up to $500 in savings.

NO SECURITY DEPOSIT FOR UTILITIES

Utility security deposits can range from $100 to $200 and are an expense you can avoid simply by having good credit.

IMPROVE YOUR CREDIT SCORE TODAY

I hope you're beginning to see how improving your credit score can help you save thousands of dollars a year. It's sad but true that those who have bad credit get treated worse and charged more. You'll have a harder time getting loans, and will tend to get dinged for more unexpected fees from utilities, cell phone companies and other companies simply because you have a low credit score.

The truth is you don't have to earn more money to have more money. Simply by managing and improving your credit score, you can start to keep more of your hard-earned money!

Now that you know some of the major benefits of having a good credit score, it's time to learn how your score is calculated and how to improve it.

THE FICO CREDIT SCORE FORMULA

The FICO score is the most widely used credit score model in the United States. Basically, it scores consumers on how likely they are to pay their bills. The letters FICO, by the way, stand for Fair Isaac Corporation.

The FICO score range is between 300 and 850. A FICO score of 300 means you are very unlikely to pay your bills in full or on time. A FICO score of 850 is perfect – meaning you are very likely to pay off all your bills on time and in full.

FICO scores are reported by the credit bureaus. The three major credit bureaus are:

> - Experian (Experian.com)
> - Transunion (Transunion.com)
> - Equifax (Equifax.com)

WHAT MAKES UP YOUR FICO CREDIT SCORE SCORE

Although the exact formula for the FICO score is kept a secret, FICO has disclosed the following components which are pretty reliable and should give you a very good picture of how your credit score is calculated:

Payment History – 35%

Payment history includes whether or not you've paid your bills on time.

Amount You Owe – 30%

This metric measures how much you owe relative to your total credit limit. Generally, you should never borrow more than 30% of your credit limit to avoid having your FICO score lowered.

For example, if your credit card limit is $10,000, you should not carry a balance of more than $7,000. If you do, your score will be lowered. Carrying multiple accounts near your limit can dramatically reduce your credit score.

Length of Credit History – 15%

This measures how long your average account has been open – the longer, the better.

Opening lots of new accounts and closing old accounts can lower your credit score.

Types of Credit You're Using – 10%

This measures the kinds of debt you have. If you only have credit card debt, that's not so good. Mortgages and car loans are deemed as "safer" and therefore increase your credit score relative to credit card debt.

This is a small part of the credit score formula, so you can still have a great credit score if you only have credit card debt, but you will have an even higher score if you maintain a mortgage or car loan as well.

New Credit – 10%

This metric measures how much new credit you have and have applied for recently.

Avoid applying for too many new lines of credit at the same time, especially credit cards.

Why Your FICO Score Is Important

Before your start shopping for a new home, be sure to check out your credit score. In the past, a 720 could get you the best rates available, but not anymore.

The bar has now been raised to 750 or higher for getting the best rates. You can take steps to improve your credit score, but you need to know where you stand first. That means you'll need to get your own credit report.

By law, you are entitled to one free credit report a year from each of the credit reporting agencies, Equifax, TransUnion and Experian. You may also receive a free report anytime that you have been turned down for credit. Be sure to obtain a copy of the credit denial page from the creditor to prove you were turned down.

Once you receive your credit reports, check them carefully for errors that could affect your score. Look for accounts that may not belong to you. Look for accounts that may show delinquencies that did not occur. Credit bureaus are required to investigate disputed items, usually within 30 days. Many people find errors on their credit reports! That's why it's so important to check them and fix any errors to maintain your good credit standing.

You can order all three reports at once or you can stagger them out over the year to monitor any corrections that have been made. But, if you plan to refinance within the next few months, order all three credit reports now. All lenders will review your credit reports thoroughly so it is important to make corrections before you apply for a new loan.

Be sure to buy your credit score when you order the credit reports because that is not included on free reports. When you obtain your free credit report from Equifax you can buy your FICO for $7.95.

You can also order your score from Fair Isaac's website[1]. True Credit is TransUnion's website. Prices range from $15.95 for a FICO score and one credit report to $47.85 for all three scores and reports. Once you know where you are with your score you can take steps to improve it.

The cheapest and best option in my opinion is just to go to CreditKarma[2] and get your report for free. Almost every other site will try to sign you up for a monthly program for $15 a month or try to charge you in some other way to get credit information, even if they advertise "free credit reports." Avoid these costly traps and scams! CreditKarma is a truly free option that works very well. You can see your score anytime you want and not pay a dime for it.

Always remember that requesting your own credit report does not impact your credit score.

---

[1] http://www.myfico.com
[2] http://www.creditkarma.com

PAY YOUR BILLS ON TIME

Your payment history counts for 35% of your score. A late payment can stay on your report for up to seven years. Being late on a two dollar payment last month is more damaging to your score than a three year old bankruptcy! When it comes to maintaining a good credit score, it's the little things that matter most.

The older the late payments are, the less effect they will have on your score. The last 24 months are the most important. That's both good and bad news. If your score is very low right now, you can increase it dramatically in a short period of time by paying all your bills on time and following the other steps in this book.

REDUCE YOUR DEBT

The amount of debt you have outstanding as a percentage of your available credit limits accounts for 30% of your score.

If you have a credit card with a $10,000 limit and a balance of $5,000 your "credit utilization" is 50%. Your credit score reflects the debt ratio for each of your cards as well as the ratio for your overall debt.

Reducing your credit utilization is one of the most effective ways to improve your score. Reduce your individual and total balances to under 30% of your available credit to get the maximum improvement in your credit score.

Don't Open Several New Accounts

Opening new accounts to improve your credit utilization does not work *if you already have at least three revolving accounts*. Opening several new accounts will hurt your score more than it would help. Instead, you're better off calling your credit card company and asking them to increase your limit. This can reduce your utilization without hurting your credit score as much as opening new accounts.

If you apply for a new credit card or other type of loan, the lender will request your credit record and that inquiry will show on your report. Five or six of these inquiries and it will hurt your score dramatically.

Likewise, you should not close any open accounts you have. Just keep whatever accounts you have open and do your best to pay your bills on time to increase your FICO score.

Credit History

The length of your credit history counts for 15% of your FICO score. This means that keeping your oldest credit card accounts open can help you improve your score, and the earlier you start using credit, the better your score will be over time.

WHAT YOU NEED YOUR CREDIT SCORE FOR

It's important that you understand what you need your credit score for. A good score can help when applying for a mortgage, auto loans, credit cards, business loans and other types of credit.

Some strategies, although they do not directly affect your credit score, will help you get a mortgage easier. Therefore, you will find tips in this book that will make getting a mortgage even easier without affecting your credit score.

It's important to plan ahead for major loans such as mortgages and auto loans. With proper planning ahead of time, you can dramatically raise your credit score using the strategies in this book and make sure to get the best possible rate and terms on your loan.

For a mortgage loan, seven years is the ideal time to plan ahead! But even if you don't have the luxury of planning that far in advance, you'll still find these strategies helpful.

33 Ways To Raise Your
Credit Score

Here is the list of 33 ways to raise your credit score. Some of these strategies will help you see an immediate increase in your credit score while others will take some time.

1. The Recency Principle

When calculating your credit score, the most emphasis is placed on recent information. For example, a late payment one month ago has more effect on your score than a late payment a year ago. Therefore, time will gradually repair bad credit; every month that passes helps your score if you pay your bills on time. There are many ways to increase your credit score quickly, but the only way to increase it permanently is to pay your bills on time and let time heal any old wounds such as missed payments or bankruptcy.

2. CLOSING ACCOUNTS

One way to raise your credit score is by having three to five open credit card accounts, with each of them having very low balances. However, if you already have more than 5 credit cards, don't close any of your open accounts unless the terms are really bad (like a high annual fee). If the terms are bad, instead of closing the account, call the credit card company and ask them to waive your annual fee or give you a different card without an annual fee.

Closing an account will lower your credit score by reducing your overall available credit and debt ratios. Therefore, only close your account as a last resort.

For example, if you have $60,000 in available credit and you're using $30,000, closing an "unused" credit card account and lowering your available credit to $50,000 will lower your credit score because your debt ratio got worse. If you must close an account, call up the credit card company on another account that you plan to keep open and ask them to raise your limit to make up for the lost credit availability.

3. ISOLATED EVENT VS. HABITUAL OFFENDER

One isolated delinquent payment isn't very damaging, but frequent delinquent payments signals a red flag that you are a habitual late payer which will drastically lower your credit score. Also, sporadic late payments (a 30 day late last month and a 30 day late three months ago) are more damaging than successive late payments (successive 30 day late payments are called "a rolling 30" and it counts as only one late payment).

This is because, if you're late multiple times in a row, agencies just assume you're going through a tough cash crunch. But if you're late and then on time and then late and then on time, it shows that you have poor financial habits and hurts your score even more. Consistency is key when it comes to raising your credit score!

This consistency principle is one reason why it's so important to manage your accounts wisely!

Forgetting to pay a credit card bill on time, especially if it happens more than once, can be more damaging to your credit score than not paying for several months in a row because you lost your job.

4. COLLECTIONS

Late payments and collection accounts will significantly lower your credit score. Collections and charge-offs are especially damaging. Even after a collection has been paid off with a zero balance, the fact that it is on your report will significantly lower your score for several years.

Credit agencies don't look at your payment amount. All they care about is that your payments are on time or not, and how delinquent they were if not paid on time.

5. DELINQUENCY SEVERITY

The later you are in making a payment, the lower your score will be. Credit agencies measure in 30, 60 and 90 day increments. A 90-day delinquency is far worse than a 30-day delinquency and will lower your score accordingly.

This is why you have to understand how the system works! For example, late payments on a mortgage that are less than 30 days late are not reported. Therefore, it may be better to avoid paying your mortgage and pay your credit cards on time if you can pay the mortgage within that 30-day window.

Utility companies do not report late payments, unless of course they turn you over to collections. If you have to be late on something, be late with utilities! Just make sure you pay the account fully when you do make up for it.

6. BANKRUPTCY

Chapter 7 and Chapter 13 bankruptcies both lower your credit score equally.

More points are **not** awarded for debt reorganization through a Chapter 13 filing.

7. ACCOUNT HISTORY

Your credit score increases the longer an account is open and the more payments you make. That's why taking a new auto loan (installment credit) will lower your score at first, because it's a new account and because the balance in proportion to the limit is very high. Over time, that loan will actually improve your credit score assuming you pay on time consistently.

If you're planning on buying a house, you should wait until after your home loan is closed before taking out a loan for furniture, appliances, automobiles, boats or any other kinds of loans. That way, you will get the best rate possible on your mortgage. If you want a low mortgage rate and you're expecting to buy a home within six months, don't open any new credit accounts until your home loan is closed!

8. GETTING AN 800+ CREDIT SCORE

If you're going for perfect credit and want to maintain a score above 800, ideally you should have only three open accounts. But there are some specialized loans where you would need up to five open accounts with a reporting history of at least 24 months.

Having a credit score in the 750 to 780 range is really excellent credit and will generally qualify you for the best rate on any mortgage loan.

9. AVOID THE CREDIT LIMIT

High credit balances near the limit will lower your score, even if you have never once missed a payment. Therefore, it is better to have several accounts with small balances than one or two accounts with large balances.

You should maintain all your balances between 0% - 30% of the allowed limit for the best credit score. There is a modest hit to score at a 50% balance compared to the credit limit. There is a major hit to score at a 75% or higher balance.

If balances are carried for some time at 75% or higher it will be impossible to maintain a credit score over 700.

10. MAXING OUT

Any account that is maxed out repeatedly month after month will lower your score, even if you pay it off every month without being late or carrying a balance. The credit monitoring system will only recognize balances under 30% at the time your credit is pulled for the best score!

The easiest solution is to get a credit limit raised and only borrow up to the 30% limit. Just call your credit card company and most of the time they will gladly raise your credit limit.

11. DEBT TO INCOME RATIO

Credit agencies aren't allowed to use your income to calculate your credit risk so your debt to income ratio does **not** affect your credit score. So even if you have a high income and can afford to have a lot of debt, your credit score will still be lowered if you carry high balances or if you have more than three open credit card accounts.

12. REVOLVING CREDIT

If you don't have any revolving credit (credit cards), your FICO score will be lower than it should be. Your credit report should include at least one account which has been open for six months or more to get a higher score. The ideal number of revolving accounts is ***three***.

You have to actually use your revolving credit too! Not using your credit cards in the past six months will "delete your basis" meaning that it will lower your credit score because inactive revolving credit accounts don't help your score.

13. MORTGAGE APPLICATIONS

When you apply for a mortgage loan, your mortgage payment history is weighted much more heavily than credit cards, installment loans or other accounts.

Do everything you can to avoid being more than 30 days delinquent on your mortgage payment to avoid a huge hit to your credit score.

14. PAYMENT HISTORY

Credit card payment history (revolving credit) has a heavier weighting on your credit score than installment loans. Therefore, it is better to pay down credit cards before paying down installment or auto loans.

15. FINANCE COMPANY LOANS

Having a finance company loan on your credit report will lower your credit score even if you pay on time. Having two finance company loans is worse; having three or more is worse still.

A regular auto loan is not considered to be in this category.

Beware of furniture companies, electronics companies, lumber yards, and other companies who set up financing through 3rd party finance companies. These types of loans should only be used as a last resort as they will damage your credit while active even if you pay them on time.

16. DEBT MANAGEMENT COMPANIES

Debt management companies and credit counseling firms reported on your credit file may significantly lower your credit score. Many creditors will report your payments as being late the entire time you are in credit counseling because they do not receive full payments each month. Avoid debt management companies to keep your score high.

17. REPOSSESSION

Anytime you go through a repossession, that creates a huge ding for your credit score. I highly recommend doing whatever you can to avoid a repossession as it can be incredibly damaging to your credit score for an extended period of time. It doesn't matter to the credit agencies if your spouse didn't pay the bills or there were extenuating circumstances.

18. CLOSING ACCOUNTS

Never close all your credit card accounts because it will lower your score significantly. It's best to keep your oldest credit card accounts open to improve your score. It's fine if you maintain a zero balance just to keep your accounts open, although it's better to use your revolving credit regularly.

The older your credit accounts, the more they will help improve your score. If you feel you must close an account, it's best to close your newest accounts first.

It's best to use revolving credit at least every six months to avoid deleting your basis. Don't pay for everything you buy with cash when you can use credit. Just make sure to pay off your account each month because carrying balances on revolving accounts (credit cards) does not build credit. Paying on time each month is what will increase your credit score.

Many consumers have found that using only one credit card to build credit can be a lot easier to manage. That way, you don't have to check 5 or 6 different accounts every month, and you minimize your risks of forgetting to pay a bill or making a billing mistake.

If you only have one account you use regularly to help build credit, it's easier to manage and can give you the benefits of maintaining credit without getting out of hand.

19. RATE SHOPPING

There's no problem with rate shopping. If you do shop for rates, it won't hurt your score if you do it right.

Here's the rule every consumer should know: ***all mortgage loan inquiries and auto loan inquiries within a 14-day period are treated as one inquiry.***

When the credit agencies see multiple inquiries during one or two weeks, they simply assume you're shopping for a single home or just one car at a time, so you won't lower your credit score simple by shopping for better rates if you do all your rate shopping in one or two weeks.

However, there can be an exception. If some of your inquiries are before and some are after the date of the credit bureaus' monthly update, your rate shopping may be treated as two inquiries.

The credit agency updates usually occur around the third week of the month—starting the 24th or 25th of the month. So it's best to shop for rates for a mortgage or auto loan between the 27th and the 20th of the month, avoiding the week of the 21st to 26th just to be safe.

Avoiding multiple inquiries on your report is a simple way to improve your credit score.

20. MULTIPLE INQUIRIES

If you have multiple inquiries from credit card companies, it will lower your score. This is because it shows you might be trying to get into a lot more debt quickly.

Even though credit card companies will try to suck you in with their discounts, deals, points and perks for applying for a credit card, avoid it! It will only lower your credit score, and if you do it 5 or 6 times in a year, the hit to your credit will be significant. Never do more than 2 credit card applications in a single month to avoid a serious drop in your score.

21. AGE

Your age is not a factor in credit approval but the age of your accounts is a factor. That's why it's best to just open up to 3 credit card accounts and keep them for a very long time to maximize your score.

22. RENT

Rent does not appear on your credit report. But when you apply for a mortgage, the lender will request a verification of your rent payment history and consider it heavily in the decision to grant a loan. Always pay your rent on time if you're trying to apply for a mortgage in the next few years.

Make sure to keep all of your rent payment records for at least two years if you plan on applying for a mortgage. Most banks now provide a picture of your checks and that should be fine to establish proof of your rent payment history. Never pay cash for your rent! Cash receipts are not accepted by most lenders. Always pay your rent with a check.

23. Negative Report History

Negative marks on your credit report such as delinquent payments, collections and bankruptcy decay over time. This means, the longer it's been since a negative hit on your report, the higher your score will be and the less the effect of that negative incident.

If you've made some mistakes handling your credit in the past, the best thing to do is just start paying your bills on time and make up for it.

24. Paying Off One Card With Another

Paying off one credit card with another you just opened and then another in a rotating fashion does not look good to creditors. Some people call this credit surfing, and it will lower your score significantly because of multiple credit card inquiries and the short length of time the accounts are open.

25. GETTING A FREE CREDIT REPORT

You are legally entitled to request a copy of your own credit report from a credit bureau without it affecting your score. I recommend CreditKarma[3] because it's fast, easy and truly free.

26. CREDIT CARD SOLICITATIONS

Credit card companies and insurance companies look at your credit file to determine who to mail solicitations to. This does not affect your credit score but it does mean a lot of junk mail and credit card offers! You can request to be excluded from these solicitations.

Remember that not only finance companies look at your credit score, but employers and insurance firms do too.

27. MARRIED COUPLES HAVE TWO SCORES

Everyone has their own individual score. So if you're married, both you and your spouse have a separate credit score. Make sure both spouses have some credit established in their own name. Credit accounts may be held jointly in both names or individually.

You can be put on an account as an "authorized user." This type of account can be excluded from the debt

---

[3] http://www.creditkarma.com

THE FICO CREDIT SCORE FORMULA

ratio which will help your score but it can hurt the borrower if they need an extra credit line because it still shows as an extra account on your report.

28. MULTIPLE NAMES OR ADDRESSES

Having several names and addresses for yourself on a credit report will lower your score. Most often, this happens if you have moved a lot within the past seven years or if you have credit in multiple names, such as: John Smith, John C. Smith, J. Smith, and Johnny Smith. Remove any extra names and addresses from your accounts and your credit score could go up 20-30 points overnight!

29. PENALTIES

Any late payments and collections will remain on your credit report for seven (7) years. Bankruptcies will remain on your credit report for up to ten (10) years. However, unpaid tax liens and civil judgments may remain on your credit report forever! That's why it's so important to pay contested accounts current and then fight to receive a refund. If you are judged to be right, you will get your money back. If you are judged to be incorrect, your credit will be severely damaged during the time of your protest, because your balance due was pending payment.

30. OCCUPATIONAL HAZARDS

Your profession does not affect your credit score. However, some institutions disfavor certain ones because of past history with late payments. Occupations which have unstable income, periods of no income, seasonal work and frequent job changes tend to be in disfavor. This would include farm work, some construction jobs, landscaping and other similar seasonal occupations. In addition, some lenders charge an extra fee to self-employed borrowers because self-employment carries a higher credit risk factor.

31. ESTABLISHING NEW CREDIT

When you are first trying to establish credit, it is easier to open a department store card or gasoline card than it is to open a bank credit card. Just make sure the new card company reports to a credit bureau so that you can start building up your credit history.

32. THE BANK LOAN TRICK

You can take out a small personal loan at a bank and deposit the money into a savings account at the same bank as collateral for the loan in order to help get credit established. The account must report for at least six months to be effective. Be sure that the loan is with a "reporting" bank. It is no help to have a loan with a bank that doesn't even report to a credit bureau!

33. FORECLOSURE

A mortgage foreclosure is even more damaging to your credit score than a bankruptcy in the eyes of a mortgage lender. If you have to choose between bankruptcy or foreclosure and you wish to buy a house in the next 7 years, it's better to go with bankruptcy in terms of improving your chances of getting the mortgage you want.

How To Dispute
An Error On Your
Credit Report

The best resource for information about how to dispute errors on your credit report is the FTC. As it says on their website[4]:

> *"Under the FCRA, both the credit reporting company and the information provider (that is, the person, company, or organization that provides information about you to a credit reporting company) are responsible for*

---

[4] http://www.consumer.ftc.gov/articles/0151-disputing-errors-credit-reports

correcting inaccurate or incomplete information in your report. To take advantage of all your rights under this law, contact the credit reporting company and the information provider.

STEP ONE

Tell the credit reporting company, in writing, what information you think is inaccurate. Include copies (NOT originals) of documents that support your position.

In addition to providing your complete name and address, your letter should clearly identify each item in your report you dispute, state the facts and explain why you dispute the information, and request that it be removed or corrected.

You may want to enclose a copy of your report with the items in question circled. Send your letter by certified mail, "return receipt requested," so you can document what the credit reporting company received. Keep copies of your dispute letter and enclosures.

Credit reporting companies must investigate the items in question — usually within 30 days — unless they consider your dispute frivolous. They also must forward all the relevant data you provide about the inaccuracy to the organization that provided the information. After the information provider receives notice of a dispute from the credit reporting company, it must investigate, review the relevant information, and report the results back to the credit reporting company. If the information provider finds the disputed information is inaccurate, it must notify all three nationwide credit reporting companies so they can correct the information in your file.

When the investigation is complete, the credit reporting company must give you the results in writing and a free copy of your report if the dispute results in a change. This free report does not count as your annual free report. If an item is changed or deleted, the credit reporting company cannot put the disputed information back in your file unless the information provider verifies that it is accurate and complete. The credit reporting company also must send you written notice that includes the name, address, and phone number of the information provider.

If you ask, the credit reporting company must send notices of any corrections to anyone who received your report in the past six months. You can have a corrected copy of your report sent to anyone who received a copy during the past two years for employment purposes.

If an investigation doesn't resolve your dispute with the credit reporting company, you can ask that a statement of the dispute be included in your file and in future reports. You also can ask the credit reporting company to provide your statement to anyone who received a copy of your report in the recent past. You can expect to pay a fee for this service.

STEP TWO

Tell the creditor or other information provider, in writing, that you dispute an item. Be sure to include copies (NOT originals) of documents that support your position. Many providers specify an address for disputes. If the provider reports the item to a credit reporting company, it must include a notice of your dispute. And if you are correct — that is, if the information is found to be inaccurate — the information provider may not report it again.

About Your File

Your credit file may not reflect all your credit accounts. Although most national department store and all-purpose bank credit card accounts will be included in your file, not all creditors supply information to credit reporting companies: some local retailers, credit unions, travel, entertainment, and gasoline card companies are among the creditors that don't.

When negative information in your report is accurate, only the passage of time can assure its removal. A credit reporting company can report most accurate negative information for seven years and bankruptcy information for 10 years. Information about an unpaid judgment against you can be reported for seven years or until the statute of limitations runs out, whichever is longer. There is no time limit on reporting: information about criminal convictions; information reported in response to your application for a job that pays more than $75,000 a year; and information reported because you've applied for more than $150,000 worth of credit or life insurance. There is a standard method for calculating the seven-year reporting period. Generally, the period runs from the date that the event took place."

Raise Your Score Now!

O kay, now that you know 33 ways to improve your credit score and you know how to file a claim to get rid of any errors on your credit report, it's time to put this information into action!

If you haven't already, get your credit report and then follow this simple exercise to put it all into action.

Step 1 - Grab a Notebook and Pen

Step 2 - Write Down Which Methods Will Apply To You

Not all 33 strategies might work for you. So write down the ones that do apply to you so you remember to actually do them.

Step 3. Take Action

Which steps can you implement right now? If you have to write a letter to fix an error on your report or call your credit card companies to raise your limits, do it now!

Step 4. Don't Stop Until You're Done

Keep your list on you and don't give up until you've raised your score to the levels you need to get the loans and credit you deserve.

CONNECT WITH TOM

Thank you so much for taking the time to read this book. I'm excited for you to start your path to improving your credit score and getting your financial life in order.

If you have any questions of any kind, feel free to contact me at:
www.tckpublishing.com/contact

You can follow me on Twitter: @JuiceTom

And connect with me on Facebook:
www.tckpublishing.com/facebook

You can check out my publishing blog for the latest updates here:
www.tckpublishing.com

I'm wishing you the best of health, happiness and success!

Here's to you!

Tom Corson-Knowles

ABOUT THE AUTHOR

TOM CORSON-KNOWLES is the #1 Amazon best-selling author of *The Kindle Publishing Bible* and *How To Make Money With Twitter*, among others. He lives in Kapaa, Hawaii. Tom loves educating and inspiring other entrepreneurs to succeed and live their dreams.

Learn more at:

www.amazon.com/author/business

Get the free Kindle publishing and marketing video training series from Tom here:
www.ebookpublishingschool.com

OTHER BOOKS BY TOM CORSON-KNOWLES

Destroy Your Distractions

Email Marketing Mastery

The Book Marketing Bible: 39 Proven Ways to Build Your Author Platform and Promote Your Books on a Budget

Schedule Your Success: How to Master the One Key Habit That Will Transform Every Area of Your Life

You Can't Cheat Success! How The Little Things You Think Aren't Important Are The Most Important of All

Guest Blogging Goldmine

Rules of the Rich: 28 Proven Strategies for Creating a Healthy, Wealthy and Happy Life and Escaping the Rat Race Once and for All

Systemize, Automate, Delegate: How to Grow a Business While Traveling, on Vacation and Taking Time Off

The Kindle Publishing Bible: How To Sell More Kindle eBooks On Amazon

The Kindle Writing Bible: How To Write a Bestselling Nonfiction Book From Start to Finish

The Kindle Formatting Bible: How to Format Your eBook for Kindle Using Microsoft Word

How To Make Money With Twitter

101 Ways To Start A Business For Less Than $1,000

Facebook For Business Owners: Facebook Marketing For Fan Page Owners and Small Businesses

How to Reduce Your Debt Overnight: A Simple System to Eliminate Credit Card and Consumer Debt

The Network Marketing Manual: Work From Home And Get Rich In Direct Sales

Dr. Corson's Top 5 Nutrition Tips

The Vertical Gardening Guidebook: How To Create Beautiful Vertical Gardens, Container Gardens and Aeroponic Vertical Tower Gardens at Home

INDEX

P

R

S

T

U

Z

61850547R00038

Made in the USA
Middletown, DE
16 January 2018